D1030515

Bald Eagles

Victoria Blakemore

vblakemore.author@gmail.com

Copyright info/picture credits

Cover, davidevison/AdobeStock; Page 3, viewsonic99/Pixabay; Page 5, skeeze/Pixabay; Page 7, the3cats/Pixabay; Page 9, skeeze/Pixabay; Pages 10-11, tpsdave/Pixabay; Page 13, Nadeem/Pixabay; Page 15, Tpedersen/Pixabay; Page 17, Barni1/Pixabay; Page 19, skeeze/Pixabay; Page 21, skeeze/Pixabay; Page 23; skeeze/Pixabay; Page 25, tpsdave/Pixabay; Page 27, davidevison/AdobeStock; Page 29, skeeze/Pixabay; Page 31, skeeze/Pixabay; Page 33, skeeze/Pixabay

Table of Contents

What Are Bald Eagles?

Bald eagles are large birds.

They are a special kind of

bird called a raptor.

Raptors have special

features to help them hunt.

Other raptors include owls,

hawks, and falcons.

Bald eagles are actually not
bald. They have white feathers
on their head.

Size

Bald eagles can grow to be as tall as three feet. They often weigh between ten and fourteen pounds.

Female bald eagles are usually larger than male bald eagles.

A bald eagle's **wingspan**

can be over eight feet long.

Physical Characteristics

Bald eagles are known for their brown and black feathers. They have white feathers on their head.

Bald eagles have sharp **talons** on their feet. They are used for grabbing and holding on to prey.

Bald eagles have a hooked beak. The curved shape allows them to easily eat prey.

Habitat

Bald eagles usually live in forests with tall trees. They prefer to live in areas that are near water, such as rivers, marshes, or lakes.

Some bald eagles **migrate** to warmer areas when it gets cold.

Range

Bald eagles are only found in

North America.

Most bald eagles are found in

Alaska and Canada.

11

Diet

Bald eagles are **carnivores**, which means that they eat meat.

Their diet is made up mostly of fish. They also eat small animals like rabbits, crabs, and reptiles.

Bald eagles swoop down from above and catch prey with their talons.

Bald eagles can carry about four pounds with their talons. They sometimes bring food back to the nest to eat.

Bald eagles can also be **scavengers**. They are often seen taking food from other animals or eating food animals leave behind.

Bald eagles sometimes eat a
lot of food at once. Then they
can go for days or weeks
without food.

Communication

Bald eagles communicate with each other through sound and movement. Sound is often used between mothers and eaglets.

They may tilt their head, flap their wings, or crouch down when they feel threatened.

Bald eagles can chirp,

whistle, and make

high-pitched cries.

Movement

Bald eagles often fly at about thirty miles per hour. When they are diving, they can reach speeds of over fifty miler per hour.

When flying from **perch** to perch, bald eagles do not need to fly as fast.

Bald eagles rarely flap their

wings when they are flying.

They usually glide and soar

through the air.

Nests

Bald eagles build very large nests out of sticks and grasses. Their nests are some of the biggest bird nests that exist.

They are usually built in tall trees. Bald eagles that migrate usually return to the same nest every year.

The largest bald eagle nest

ever found was in Florida. It

weighed over 4,000 pounds.

Eaglets

Eagles lay up to three eggs at a time. Once the eggs hatch, the eaglets have soft, white feathers.

The parents feed the eaglets for the first three months. Then they are old enough to fly and feed themselves.

Eaglets change colors as they grow. They will look like adult eagles by the time they are five years old.

Lifespan

In the wild, bald eagles usually live between fifteen and twenty years. The oldest bald eagle on record in the wild was thirty-eight years old.

In **captivity**, they often live between twenty and thirty years.

National Symbol

Bald eagles are a national symbol of the United States.

Benjamin Franklin did not want the bald eagle to be our national symbol because they steal from other animals. He thought it should be a wild turkey.

Bald eagles represent freedom, which is important to the United States.

Population

Bald eagles were listed as **endangered** for many years. Many people were hunting them. **Pesticides** were also causing problems with bald eagle eggs.

Now, there are thought to be over 250,000 bald eagles in the wild.

In 2007, bald eagles were taken

off the endangered species list.

Helping Bald Eagles

Bald eagle populations have grown, but they are still at risk. Special laws have been written to help protect bald eagles.

Certain pesticides have been banned in the United States to help protect bald eagles.

People can't build too close

to bald eagle nesting sites.

This helps to protect their

habitat from noise and

destruction.

Bird sanctuaries also help

bald eagles that have been

hurt. They help them get

better so they can be

released back into the wild.

Glossary

Captivity: when animals are kept by people, not in the wild

Carnivore: an animal that eats meat

Endangered: at risk of becoming extinct

Migrate: to move from one place to another

Perch: a branch that a bird sits on

Pesticide: a chemical used to kill insects that harm plants or crops

Scavenger: an animal that eats dead animals it finds

Talons: sharp, curved claws

Wingspan: the distance between the tips of a birds wings

About the Author

Victoria Blakemore is a first grade

teacher in Southwest Florida with a

passion for reading.

You can visit her at

www.elementaryexplorers.com

Also in This Series

Also in This Series

CPSIA information can be obtained
at www.ICGtesting.com
Printed in the USA
LVHW071638071021
699830LV00005B/315